D1239197

SandCastle

Keeping the Peace

Coping with Anger

Pam Scheunemann

Consulting Editor, Diane Craig, M.A./Reading Specialist

ABDO
Publishing Company

Published by ABDO Publishing Company, 4940 Viking Drive, Edina, Minnesota 55435.

Printed in the United States.

Credits
Edited by: Pam Price
Curriculum Coordinator: Nancy Tuminelly
Cover and Interior Design and Production: Mighty Media
Photo Credits: BananaStock Ltd., Brand X Pictures, Corbis Images, Digital Vision, Image Source, PhotoDisc, Stockbyte

Library of Congress Cataloging-in-Publication Data

Scheunemann, Pam, 1955-
    Coping with anger / Pam Scheunemann.
       p. cm. -- (Keeping the peace)
    Includes index.
    Summary: Describes ways of coping with anger that help to maintain the peace.
    ISBN 1-59197-559-X
    1. Anger--Juvenile literature. 2. Conduct of life--Juvenile literature. 3. Peace--Juvenile literature. [1. Anger. 2. Peace.] I. Title.

BF575.A5S34 2004
152.4'7--dc22
                                                                        2003057785

SandCastle™ books are created by a professional team of educators, reading specialists, and content developers around five essential components that include phonemic awareness, phonics, vocabulary, text comprehension, and fluency. All books are written, reviewed, and leveled for guided reading, early intervention reading, and Accelerated Reader® programs and designed for use in shared, guided, and independent reading and writing activities to support a balanced approach to literacy instruction.

Let Us Know

After reading the book, SandCastle would like you to tell us your stories about reading. What is your favorite page? Was there something hard that you needed help with? Share the ups and downs of learning to read. We want to hear from you! To get posted on the ABDO Publishing Company Web site, send us e-mail at:

sandcastle@abdopub.com

SandCastle Level: Transitional

Learning to cope
with your anger
keeps the peace.

It's normal to be angry sometimes.

A peacekeeper learns ways to handle her anger.

It is never okay to hurt someone or something when you are angry.

Bill needs to learn how to cope with his anger.

It is important to express your anger without hurting others.

Sam talks to his dad about what is making him angry.

Learn to calm down
when you start feeling
angry.

Mary decides to take a
time-out when she gets
angry.

It helps to write down your feelings when you are angry.

Wendy describes how she feels about a fight with her brother.

Exercise can help you become less angry.

Jason kicks his ball to let off a little steam when he's angry.

People who are angry may say things they don't really mean.

Grace and John take time to think before talking to each other.

People express their anger in many ways.

Ali makes a drawing to show how she feels.

Rachel doesn't let little things upset her.

She is much happier now that she can cope with her anger.

What can you do to keep the peace?

Glossary

anger. a strong feeling of displeasure or unhappiness

calm. to become quiet or peaceful

cope. to face difficulties and act to overcome them

exercise. an activity you do to keep your body healthy and fit

express. to make your feelings or thoughts known through words or actions

time-out. a short break from work or play

About SandCastle™

A professional team of educators, reading specialists, and content developers created the SandCastle™ series to support young readers as they develop reading skills and strategies and increase their general knowledge. The SandCastle™ series has four levels that correspond to early literacy development in young children. The levels are provided to help teachers and parents select the appropriate books for young readers.

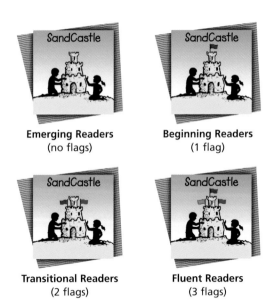

Emerging Readers
(no flags)

Beginning Readers
(1 flag)

Transitional Readers
(2 flags)

Fluent Readers
(3 flags)

These levels are meant only as a guide. All levels are subject to change.

To see a complete list of SandCastle™ books and other nonfiction titles from ABDO Publishing Company, visit **www.abdopub.com** or contact us at:

4940 Viking Drive, Edina, Minnesota 55435 • 1-800-800-1312 • fax: 1-952-831-1632